i-SPY

D0566611

at the seaside

SPY IT! SCORE IT!

Introduction

A day at the seaside! Building sandcastles; all the fun of the fair; crazy golf; windsurfing; messing about in rock pools; some fish and chips; a stick of rock; soaring sea birds; and lovely wild flowers on the cliffs. These are just a few of the joys to be had for anyone visiting the coast – the list is endless!

Whatever the time of year, there is always something interesting to i-SPY at the seaside. Next time you go to the seaside, be sure to keep your book handy when you're digging in the sand or walking along the pier. You never know what you might see next.

How to use your i-SPY book

Keep your eyes peeled for the i-SPYs in the book.

If you spy it, score it by ticking the circle or star.

Items with a star are difficult to spot so you'll have to search high and low to find them.

If there is a question and you know the answer, double your points. Answers can be found at the back of the book (no cheating, please!)

Once you score 1000 points, send away for your super i-SPY certificate. Follow the instructions on page 64 to find out how.

Open-top bus

 10 POINTS

Many seaside resorts run an open-top bus – a perfect way to see the sights, especially on a sunny day!

Cliff railway

These short railways run up and down a steep gradient from the bottom to the top of a cliff.

What is a funicular railway?

 10 POINTS

3

On the prom

TOP SPOT!

PUNCH · JUDY

PROFESSOR JOHN PULSON

Professor Pulson's
PUNCH & JUDY
SHOW
all round
childrens
entertainer
to book
telephone...
01394 460871

Punch and Judy

First seen in Britain in the 17th century,
Punch and Judy shows are normally
performed by a single 'professor', who
controls both the puppets.

25 POINTS

Beach hut

Some resorts have long lines of these little cabins.

10 POINTS

Deck chair

No seaside town would be complete without its deck chairs.

5 POINTS

Telescope

You'll often find these coin-operated telescopes at the seaside.

5 POINTS

Seaside shelter

You can enjoy the sea air in the worst of weather by sitting in one of these shelters.

10 POINTS

On the prom

Pleasure piers

Many resorts have long piers reaching out into the sea.

 10 POINTS

Theatre

The traditional theatre on a pier is a good place to see a top act or entertainer.

⭐ **15** POINTS

Funfair

Funfairs, at the end of the pier, have been popular since Victorian times.

10 POINTS

Cannon

Historic coastal defences like cannons have been recovered from old ships and set up for decoration.

⭐ **20** POINTS

Blackpool tower

Blackpool Tower opened in 1894 and was inspired by the Eiffel Tower in Paris.

25 POINTS

Grand hotel

If you're spending a holiday at a big seaside resort, you may be lucky enough to stay in one of the very luxurious hotels on the seafront.

15 POINTS

Lighthouse

The light from lighthouses used to warn sailors of dangers, such as rocks.

15 POINTS

On the beach

Boardwalk

Boardwalks are wooden structures that make it easy to walk across sand and help stop erosion.

20 POINTS

Paddling dog

Dogs enjoy a good splash about in the sea and they don't seem to mind that the water is cold.

10 POINTS

Beach cleaning

The hard work of cleaning up the beach begins, for another day of fun.

10 POINTS

Beach tent

Change into your swimwear and shelter from the wind and sun in a little tent.

5 POINTS

Windbreak

If it's blustery, these portable walls are a great way to keep the wind off.

5 POINTS

Beachcombing

Coin collectors, archaeologists, and treasure hunters may be found scanning the sand with their metal detectors.

15 POINTS

Beach sports

Wetsuit

Wetsuits keep swimmers and surfers warm in cold water.

10 POINTS

Volleyball

Some beaches have a permanent volleyball court.

15 POINTS

Kite landboard

Watch landboarders scoot along the sand on a windy day with a huge kite and a set of wheels.

20 POINTS

Cricket

A game of beach cricket is always fun.

 10 POINTS

Kite buggy

This modern sport takes full advantage of the wind as the large kite pulls the buggy along below.

TOP SPOT!

25 POINTS

Bowls

A slower game to be enjoyed by all ages.

 10 POINTS

Water sports

Canoe

Take to the sea in a canoe with a responsible adult.

 15 POINTS

Windsurfing

It takes skill and practice to balance and manoeuvre when windsurfing.

 **15** POINTS

Jet ski

Jet skis are speedy, so lifeguards use them to rescue people.

15 POINTS

Kayaking

One paddle and away you go – be sure to take an adult with you.

 20 POINTS

Surfer

Surfing takes lots of practice but hiring a board is easy!

 10 POINTS

Surf school

Learn how to surf at a surf school.

15 POINTS

Bodyboard

If surfing is too tricky, bodyboarding is also fun.

 10 POINTS

TOP SPOT!

Kitesurfer

The adventurous use the wind to propel themselves across the sea.

30 POINTS

The seaside

Pontoon

A pontoon is like a floating bridge, anchored to the seabed, that makes reaching a boat easy.

15 POINTS

Swimming platform

A floating platform, anchored to the seabed out in a bay which is safe for swimming.

25 POINTS

TOP SPOT!

TOP SPOT!

Bridge

You need to have a head for heights to walk across a bridge over a coastal ravine!

25 POINTS

Other attractions

Zoo

Some seaside towns have a zoo where you can see a variety of different animals.

 10 POINTS

Swimming pool

A nice distraction, especially if the weather is not good!

 **15** POINTS

Aquarium

Explore life beneath the waves at an aquarium.

 20 POINTS

Playing around

Swan ride

Hire one of these special pedalos and ride a swan.

xuanhuongho / Shutterstock.com

Model boat

Model boats look just like full-size ones but are much smaller.

Trampoline

You can challenge your friends to a bouncing competition!

Crazy golf

Practise your putting skills over the ramps and through the hazards of a game of crazy golf.

Swing boat

Riders have to take turns to pull on the two ropes inside the boat to make them swing backwards and forwards.

Playing around

Stefano Ember / Shutterstock.com

Miniature railway

These mini engines offer a lovely way to travel around fun parks.

15 POINTS

Donkey ride

A donkey ride is a traditional way to travel along the beach.

10 POINTS

Go-karting

If you prefer something a little faster, put your foot down.

10 POINTS

Winter fishing

You can spy hardy anglers with their beach rods whatever the weather!

 10 POINTS

Fun fishing

You don't need a lot of expensive equipment to go fishing.

10 POINTS

Catch

Many anglers put their catch back in the sea.

15 POINTS

Sand fun

Buried

It's always fun to bury someone – especially if it is an adult!

5 POINTS

Beachball

Why not have a game of beach football? Do you prefer playing on sand or grass?

5 POINTS

Sand sculpture

Sand sculptures can be of anything – use shells and seaweed to decorate it when you're done!

Sandcastle

Build one and get someone to judge whether yours is better than the one here.

Sand drawing

You don't have to build upward. You can have a lot of fun drawing in the sand with a stick.

Up in the air

Parachute displays

You might see individual or team parachute displays near the beach.

20 POINTS

Hot-air ballooning

You will sometimes see brightly-coloured balloons around our coastlines during clear days, especially in the early morning.

15 POINTS

Hang-glider

Hang-gliders jump off high cliffs and can stay in the air for hours.

15 POINTS

Red Arrows

The Royal Air Force Aerobatic Team, the Red Arrows, flies overhead in close formation with the planes releasing coloured vapour trails.

25 POINTS

Feeling peckish?

Candy floss

Yummy candy floss is always a seaside treat.

5 POINTS

Fish and chips

Fish and chips and other seafood are traditional meals at the seaside.

5 POINTS

Stick of rock

The most famous rock is peppermint, which is pink on the outside and white in the middle, with the name of the seaside town printed on it.

The name of the town is only on the ends of the stick of rock. True or false?

5 POINTS

Sweet shop

The shops along the promenade offer a huge selection of sweets.

5 POINTS

Ice cream van

After all that bouncing around, you may want to cool down with an ice cream or ice lolly.

5 POINTS

FRESHLY MADE FOR YOU!

25

Souvenirs

Shoes

Many shoes designed for the beach are made of plastic or rubber and have holes that let seawater drain out easily.

Bucket and spade

You'll need these for building a sandcastle or digging up the sand.

Inflatables

Make sure you have lots of puff to blow these up!

All the fun of the fair

Drop tower

This ride has its ups
and downs!

15 POINTS

Dodgems

You are supposed to dodge
the other cars –
not hit them!

15 POINTS

House of fun

The House of Fun has
lots of attractions
designed to
make you laugh!

15 POINTS

Merry-go-round

Traditional merry-go-rounds
were driven by steam engines,
and you can sometimes still
find them at steam fairs.

10 POINTS

*What other name is given to
merry-go-rounds, especially
in the United States?*

Chair-o-plane

These have been a favourite for many years. Chairs are suspended from a big top, which rotates. The chairs then fly outwards, like 'planes', when the ride is in motion.

25 POINTS

Roller coaster

With its speed and fast turns, the roller coaster is one of the most exciting rides of any funfair.

 20 POINTS

Helter-skelter

On a helter-skelter you slide down from the top of the tower on a special mat. 'Helter-skelter' roughly means 'disorderly haste'.

 **15** POINTS

Wheel turner

Not for the faint-hearted!

 10 POINTS

All the fun of the fair

Amusement arcade

If the weather is bad, cheer yourself up in an amusement arcade.

 10 POINTS

Token machine

Many attractions do not take cash – you will need to exchange your money for a token.

5 POINTS

Try your luck

Try your luck at winning a toy using an electronic claw.

 5 POINTS

Bingo

Who can resist a game of bingo?

 5 POINTS

For the adventurous type

Rock climb

Rock climbing on beach cliffs can be fun but only try this under supervision and when wearing the correct safety equipment.

25 POINTS

TOP SPOT!

Horse

You'll find some riding schools offer beach excursions with their ponies and horses.

20 POINTS

Cliff hike

Be careful if you go on a cliff hike above the beach – take an adult with you!

20 POINTS

Signs

Sea wash

Take care! The tide can get high in some places.

10 POINTS

Toilets

Toilets are always close at hand at the seaside.

5 POINTS

Parking tickets

Be sure to pay and display when parking.

5 POINTS

No dogs

Some beaches don't allow dogs...

 5 POINTS

Dogs on leads

...whereas some beaches accept dogs as long as they are kept on a lead.

 10 POINTS

Keep dogs on leads

Changes in level

Be careful if you see this sign. The submerged beach may suddenly drop away.

 10 POINTS

Signs and other items near the beach

Litter bin

Always put your litter in the bins provided.

 5 POINTS

Alcohol-free zone

No alcohol should be drunk on beaches with this sign.

10 POINTS

Cycle lane

Be sure to look both ways if you cross a cycle path.

 10 POINTS

Groynes

Beach groynes perform a very important role.

What is a groyne? **10** POINTS

Ferry

This is a modern ferry for carrying cars, trucks, and passengers. It can carry more than 2000 passengers and up to 650 vehicles.

15 POINTS

Yacht

Many yachts rely solely on wind power for movement.

15 POINTS

TOP SPOT!

Luxury yacht

You might see this luxury craft moored at the marina.

25 POINTS

An ocean of ships

Old ship

Britain has a long maritime history and there have been many famous sea captains and ships.

25 POINTS

Schooner

Schooners are sailing ships with at least two masts, favoured by pirates from the 16th to 18th centuries.

25 POINTS

Dinghy

Dinghies range in size. To keep the boat on an even keel, the crew can be suspended from one side on a trapeze.

15 POINTS

Cruise liner

Cruise liners are massive floating hotels that can carry thousands of guests.

20 POINTS

Boat building

Ships have to be constructed in a special 'dry dock' before being launched into the sea.

What is the traditional ceremony for launching a new ship? **10 POINTS**

Double with answer

Boat trip

15 POINTS

You will often find kiosks selling tickets for sightseeing boat trips.

Fender

5 POINTS

Some boats have traditional plastic fenders, or bumpers, hanging along the side to prevent damage.

Fishing trawler

Trawlers fish out at sea by dragging a net along the seabed to catch bottom-feeding fish.

15 POINTS

Container ship

These massive vessels carry huge amounts of cargo around the world.

10 POINTS

TOP SPOT!

Hovercraft

These spectacular vessels travel at great speeds and skim over the surface of the water on a cushion of air.

30 POINTS

Buoy

Floating buoys, attached by ropes, mark lanes to keep the harbour traffic in good order.

5 POINTS

Boat hoist

The contents of a boat will sometimes require a crane or hoist to help lift it to the shore.

10 POINTS

Bollard

A ship's mooring lines, or hawsers, are made fast (tied) to the bollard to stop it floating away.

5 POINTS

39

At the fish quay

Lobster pot

Lobster pots are distributed around the coast in order to trap lobsters.

How does the fisherman know where the pots are left?

10 POINTS

Crane

Big ships need big cranes to assist in their loading and unloading.

10 POINTS

Fishing boat

You will see lots of these small fishing boats around the coast.

10 POINTS

TOP SPOT!

Boat out of water

Boats need regular maintenance. You may see a fishing boat removed from the water getting its hull repainted, or a yacht getting scrubbed clean to remove debris.

25 POINTS

Harbour steps

Harbour steps are often slippery due to seawater and seaweed – take care on them.

5 POINTS

Low tide

At low tide you may see some boats out of water in the harbour.

5 POINTS

Nets

You might see fishing nets curled up on a trawler or laid out on the quayside.

5 POINTS

Lifeguard

On busy beaches you might see a lifeguard keeping an eye on the water.

5 POINTS

Marine rescue vehicle

This 4x4 vehicle is driven by members of Her Majesty's Coastguard.

15 POINTS

Lifeboat at sea

The Royal National Lifeboat Institution will rush to the aid of anyone in need of assistance.

20 POINTS

Rescue

Lifeguard vehicle

Many beaches have a lifeguard truck stationed on the beach.

15 POINTS

Lifeboat launch

Lifeboats can be launched very quickly from the shore down a slipway when there is an emergency.

30 POINTS

TOP SPOT!

Life buoy

A life buoy can be used as a safety aid if a swimmer is in distress.

5 POINTS

Helicopter

A coastguard helicopter can reach people in inaccessible places and whisk them to safety or hospital very quickly.

25 POINTS

Safety signs and flags

Take care

Signs like this one warn of the power of the sea.

10 POINTS

Safe swimming

These flags mean that the area is patrolled by lifeguards. You should only swim in the area between these flags.

5 POINTS

Beach safety

These signs offer a combination of safety instructions.

5 POINTS

Offshore island

Around the British coast there are offshore islands that can be seen from the seaside.

20 POINTS

Cave

You may find a natural cave in the rocks – they're often slippery though, so take care!

15 POINTS

Cliffs

Your first sight of the seaside will often be the cliffs inland from the beach.

Where are Britain's famous 'white cliffs'?

10 POINTS

Double with answer

Sand dune

Sand is blown from the beach and trapped by plants to create sand dunes.

10 POINTS

Sea arch

A sea arch can form where the waves
hollow out a cave on either side of a
headland. Eventually the two caves
meet to make the arch.

25
POINTS

Black-headed gull

This small gull forms flocks in winter. Their heads are actually dark brown, but only in summer. **5** POINTS

Fulmar

Fulmars soar elegantly on the currents of air along cliffs. **10** POINTS

Lesser black-backed gull

This gull is slightly smaller than the herring gull and has a bright yellow beak, legs and feet – and a black back. **10** POINTS

Herring gull

This is probably the gull you are most likely to see at the seaside. It has paler wings than the black-backed gull. **5** POINTS

Birds

Oystercatcher

Oystercatchers are noisy birds with large orange-red beaks.

10 POINTS

Turnstone

These wading birds prefer stony beaches to sand. Their name comes from turning over stones to find their food.

15 POINTS

Dunlin

A small starling-sized wader which forms huge flocks in winter.

10 POINTS

Shag

The shag looks similar to a cormorant but is smaller and rarely seen away from the sea. In spring, it has a crest on its head.

15 POINTS

Bird's-foot trefoil

This plant flowers throughout the summer and forms a beautiful carpet of yellow, pea-like flowers on cliff tops.

 10 POINTS

Rock samphire

This plant is grown commercially for its fleshy leaves and stems, which are sold for use in top restaurants.

 10 POINTS

Marram grass

This tough grass builds sand dunes and protects our coasts from erosion.

 5 POINTS

Wild flowers

Sea lavender

Because of its very shallow roots, sea lavender does not need much soil to grow and can live on narrow cliff ledges.

 10 POINTS

Sea holly

Sea holly is found on shingle beaches and on sand dunes – it has blue flower heads and spiky leaves.

 15 POINTS

Sea thrift

Sea thrift, or sea pink, grows in salt marshes and on sea cliffs throughout the summer.

10 POINTS

Sea campion

Sea campion flowers throughout the summer and is a variety of bladder campion, which grows along roadsides in the UK.

15 POINTS

Sea aster

Sea aster grows in similar places to thrift and flowers from July to October.

15 POINTS

Blue jellyfish

Also known as the bluefire jellyfish, individuals form chains made of tens of thousands. They are known to kill fish.

20 POINTS

By-the-wind sailor

This free-floating sea creature is easily identified by the small, stiff sail which helps it skim over the oceans.

20 POINTS

Sea urchin

Normally you will only find the hard skeleton of an urchin known as a 'test', after a gull has eaten the urchin for a meal.

15 POINTS

Mermaid's purse

Also called devil's purse, these are the egg cases of the lesser spotted dogfish, or, more unusually, of several species of shark or ray.

 20 POINTS

Periwinkle

The common periwinkle has been collected by humans as food for centuries.

 10 POINTS

Razorfish

Razorfish can reach over 20 cm long, and their empty shells are often found washed up on the tideline.

 10 POINTS

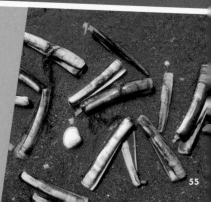

Rock pool

Blenny

Some fish get caught in rock pools when the tide goes out; others, like blennies, live in the pools.

TOP SPOT!

⭐ **25 POINTS**

Starfish

The common starfish has five arms but if in danger, it may deliberately shed one before scuttling away. It will then grow another arm.

⭐ **15 POINTS**

Sea anemone

Not a flower, but an animal! Its 'petals' are actually stinging tentacles which surround its mouth.

◯ **10 POINTS**

Squat lobster

Actually more closely related to
crabs, they are much smaller than
standard lobsters.

25
POINTS

Rock pool

Velvet crab

This is one of our largest crabs – its shell is covered by thin brown fur.

15 POINTS

Shore crab

This common shore crab is the one you are most likely to find at the seaside.

20 POINTS

Hermit crab

As hermit crabs grow, they require ever-larger empty shells which they carry on their backs.

20 POINTS

Edible crab

20 POINTS

These reddish-brown adults can reach 25 cm and weigh 3 kg. They are aggressive so be careful!

Limpet

When attacked, these conical molluscs stick to rocks like, well, limpets!

5 POINTS

Cockle

The cockle is a small member of the clam family that lives just underneath the surface of sandy beaches.

10 POINTS

Ragworm

Ragworms are often used by fishermen as bait, and they are found in muddy or gravelly conditions.

10 POINTS

Grey seal

Grey seals eat fish and can be seen at sea or on deserted winter beaches and rocks.

25 POINTS

TOP SPOT!

Whelk

Whelks move in a similar way to land snails; they creep across the sand and silt on a film of slime.

5 POINTS

Seaweeds

Bladderwrack

It gets its name from the air-filled bladders which help the fronds of the weed to float.

10 POINTS

Oarweed

10 POINTS

This type of seaweed is brown and leathery and can grow up to 3 metres long.

Do you know another name that is commonly given to it?

Knotted wrack

You can work out knotted wrack's age by counting the air bladders on a single frond – one for each year of the plant's age.

10 POINTS

Saw wrack

It gets its name from the toothed edges of the fronds.

10 POINTS

End of the day

Sunset

At the end of a wonderful day at the seaside, you might be lucky enough to see the sun go down. Seaside sunsets can be spectacular.

15
POINTS

Index

Answers: P3 Funicular, one with two cars, one going up while the other goes down so that gravity helps. **P24** Rock, False. **P27** Merry-go-round, Carousel. **P34** Groyne, a man-made barrier to prevent sand from moving down a beach. **P37** Ship launch, breaking a bottle (usually Champagne) across the bow (front of the ship). **P40** Lobster Pots, by using floats. **P47** White Cliffs, Dover. **P61** Oarweed, Kelp

i-SPY How to get your i-SPY certificate and badge

Let us know when you've become a super-spotter with 1000 points and we'll send you a special certificate and badge!

Here's what to do:

 Ask a grown-up to check your score.

 Apply for your certificate at
www.collins.co.uk/i-SPY
(if you are under the age of 13 we'll
need a parent or guardian to do this).

 We'll email your certificate and
post you a brilliant badge!